Other titles in the series:
The Crazy World of Aerobics (Bill Stott)
The Crazy World of Cats (Bill Stott)
The Crazy World of Cricket (Bill Stott)
The Crazy World of Gardening (Bill Stott)
The Crazy World of the Greens (Barry Knowles)
The Crazy World of the Handyman (Roland Fiddy)
The Crazy World of Hospitals (Bill Stott)
The Crazy World of Housework (Bill Stott)
The Crazy World of Learning to Drive (Bill Stott)
The Crazy World of Love (Roland Fiddy)
The Crazy World of Marriage (Bill Stott)
The Crazy World of the Office (Bill Stott)
The Crazy World of Photography (Bill Stott)
The Crazy World of Rugby (Bill Stott)
The Crazy World of Sailing (Peter Rigby)
The Crazy World of Sex (David Pye)

This paperback edition published simultaneously in 1992 by Exley Publications Ltd. in Great Britain, and Exley Giftbooks in the USA.
First hardback edition published in Great Britain in 1988 by Exley Publications Ltd.

Reprinted 1992 (twice) and 1993 (twice)

ISBN 1-85015-356-6

A copy of the CIP data is available from the British Library on request.

Printed in Spain by Grafo S.A., Bilbao.

Exley Publications Ltd, 16 Chalk Hill, Watford, Herts WD1 4BN, United Kingdom.
Exley Giftbooks, 359 East Main Street, Suite 3D, Mount Kisco, NY 10549, USA.

"But it's only a game!"

the CRAZY world of GOLF

Cartoons by Mike Scott

EXLEY

MT. KISCO, NEW YORK • WATFORD, UK

"Just as I thought— not as far advanced as ourselves..."

The hole that got away.

HAPPY BIRTHDAY
What could it be?

They're mostly Japanese in that hotel

The follow through...

A Scotsman at the 19th, having just scored a hole in one...

I just don't understand it – a Saturday afternoon and the course is absolutely empty!

"Oh, and I'll need some clubs—
those nice blue & gold ones will match my outfit."

I do believe he's trying to tell us something!

You mean to say your game's getting better if you hit the ball LESS often?

I say, old chap-
give me one of
those nice shiny
ones please!

Now do I call the Club President 'Sir', or 'Your Holiness'?

It's the safest place...

Ah! you've found my ball!

FOUR!
FORE?

Now a Golf Ball would really be tempting!

Members are requested
not to drink and drive!

JERICHO WELCOMES CAREFUL DRIVERS
Right lads—
after three...

WASHING BALLS IN THE SINK IS NOT ALLOWED

Bunker Shot.

...never be put off your stroke...

BEGINNERS
GOLF
CLUB

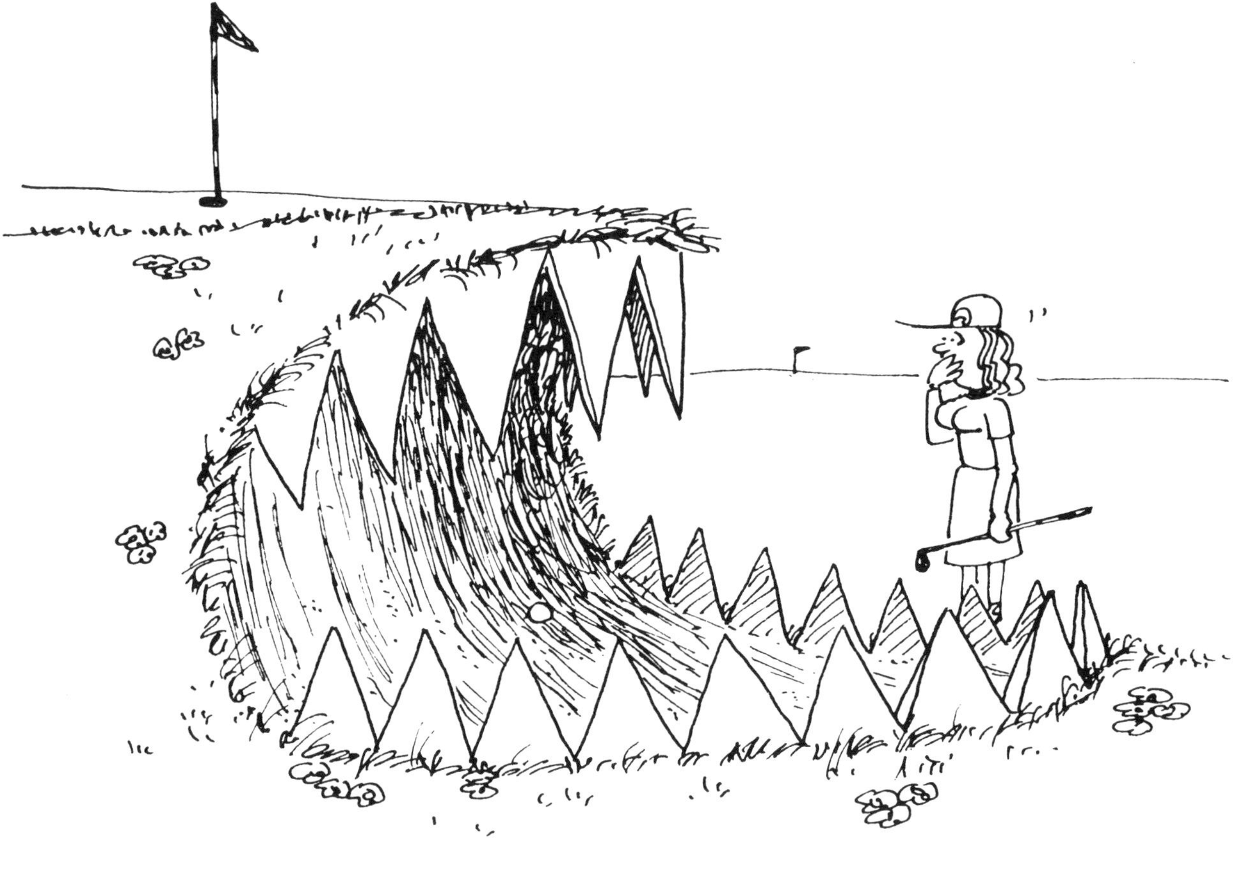

Dealing with a Water Hazard.

"I'm damned sure you forfeit a stroke for this!"

... that's the Club Pro —
he gets paid for results ...

How to deal with the Golf Club Bore.

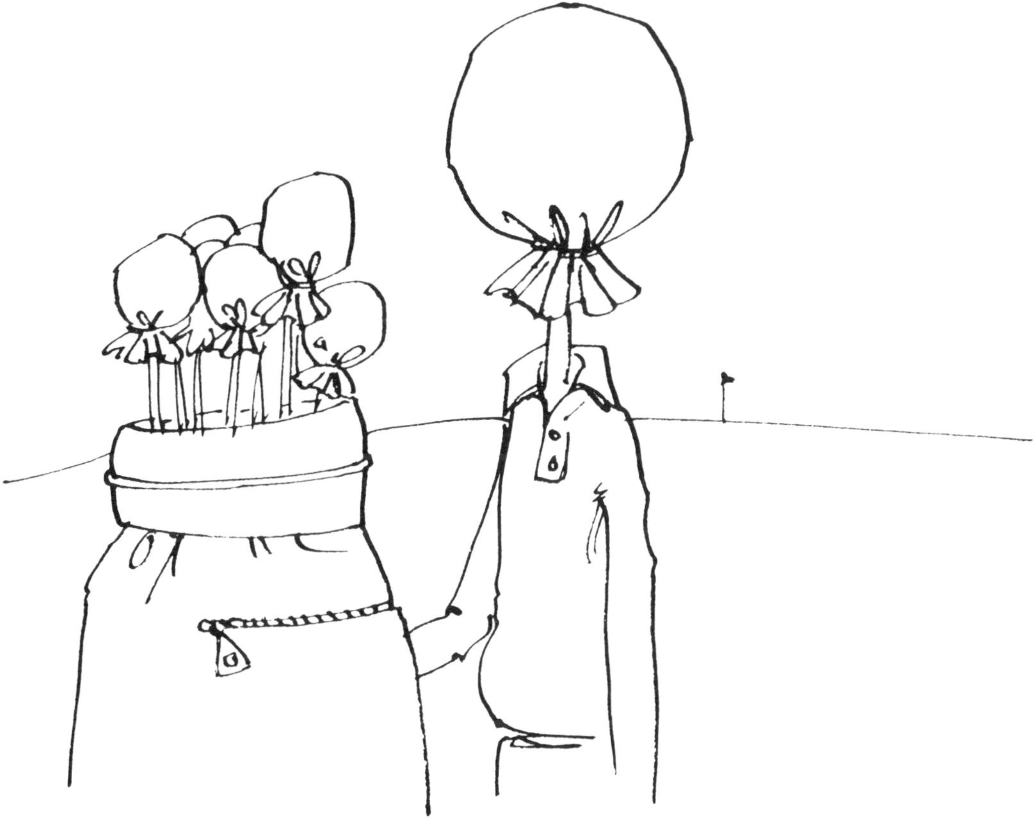

My God– Another U.F.O. Now do you believe me!

RELIEF MAP
TOILETS
TOILETS
TOILETS
TOILETS
TOILETS
TOILETS
TOILETS
TOILETS

19

Ahh! we're close to the Clubhouse now...

"He was here
a moment ago..."

Oops! Ive FLUFFED!
Well, Keep it to yousself Buddy!

Lucky? What do you mean-LUCKY?

O.K. you can have that damn Promotion!

Out of bounds…

"Pardon me pal, but can I see your Miner's Union card?"

The ·38 Iron.

"No, my son, I am not a wise hermit.
I just can't afford my Club subscriptions!"

Good old Jenkins, he just never knew when to give up.

A bender?
Exactly!

You heard – I want a divorce!
JUST MARRIED

I always dress to suit the game I expect from my opponent!

A wee saving
on Caddie fees...

Improving your game.

A distraction to a lady's game ...

... the problem solved!

Well– that was a wasted trip!
GOLF CLUB
MEMBERS
ONLY

"Look at those idiots – fishing in this weather!"

Looking for something?

WOW! you nearly lost your ball down that hole mister!

JUST MARRIED

Can't the P.M. just buy a new ball?

Have you met my handicap?

Oh him – he got a hole-in-one and kept it to himself.

CUSTOMS
..and the purpose of your visit?...

You there— have you seen
a golf ball land near here?

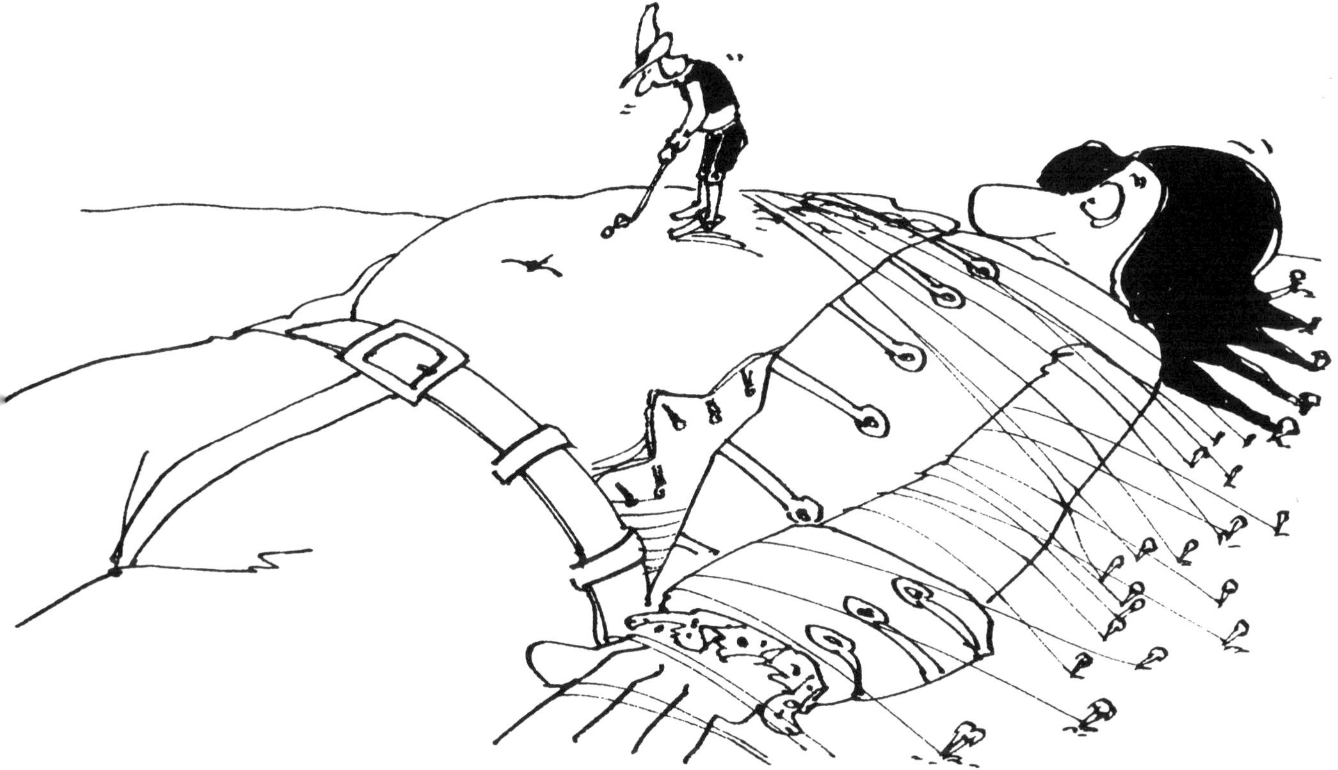

I did say try the 8 iron
but you just won't listen.

Easy doesit-
no need to rush
a super shot...

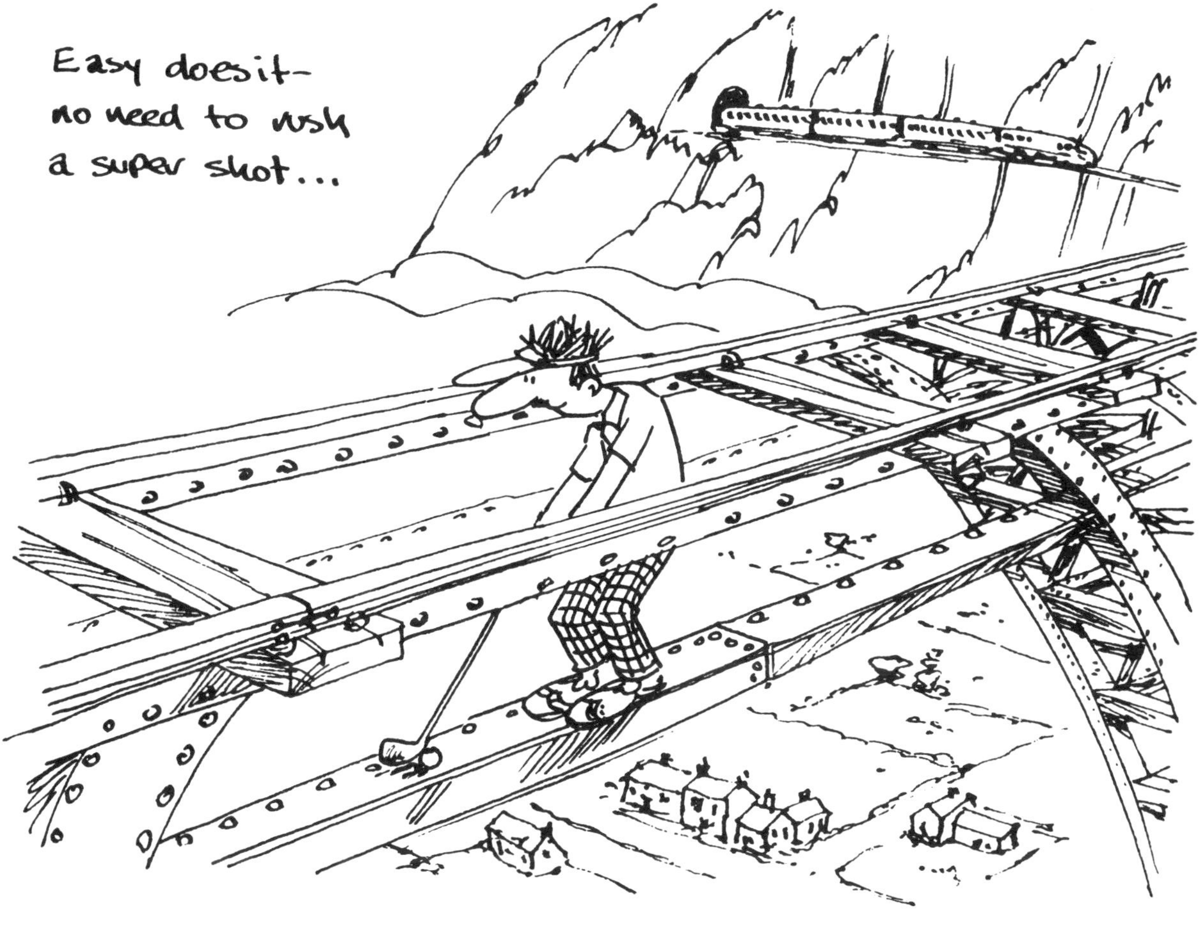

Divine Intervention...

"No, he won't be able to play as usual on Friday."

Well you'll just have to wait!

Wow! It's not what I was expecting!

Books in the "Crazy World" series

($4.99 £2.99 paperback)

The Crazy World of Aerobics (Bill Stott)
The Crazy World of Cats (Bill Stott)
The Crazy World of Cricket (Bill Stott)
The Crazy World of Gardening (Bill Stott)
The Crazy World of Golf (Mike Scott)
The Crazy World of the Greens (Barry Knowles)
The Crazy World of The Handyman (Roland Fiddy)
The Crazy World of Hospitals (Bill Stott)
The Crazy World of Housework (Bill Stott)
The Crazy World of Learning (Bill Stott)
The Crazy World of Love (Roland Fiddy)
The Crazy World of Marriage (Bill Stott)
The Crazy World of The Office (Bill Stott)
The Crazy World of Photography (Bill Stott)
The Crazy World of Rugby (Bill Stott)
The Crazy World of Sailing (Peter Rigby)
The Crazy World of Sex (David Pye)

Books in the "Mini Joke Book" series

($6.99 £3.99 hardback)

These attractive 64 page mini joke books are illustrated throughout by Bill Stott.

A Binge of Diet Jokes
A Bouquet of Wedding Jokes
A Feast of After Dinner Jokes
A Knockout of Sports Jokes
A Portfolio of Business Jokes
A Round of Golf Jokes
A Romp of Naughty Jokes
A Spread of Over-40s Jokes
A Tankful of Motoring Jokes

Books in the "Fanatics" series

($4.99 £2.99 paperback)

The **Fanatic's Guides** are perfect presents for everyone with a hobby that has got out of hand. Eighty pages of hilarious black and white cartoons by Roland Fiddy.

The Fanatic's Guide to the Bed
The Fanatic's Guide to Cats
The Fanatic's Guide to Computers
The Fanatic's Guide to Dads
The Fanatic's Guide to Diets
The Fanatic's Guide to Dogs
The Fanatic's Guide to Husbands
The Fanatic's Guide to Money
The Fanatic's Guide to Sex
The Fanatic's Guide to Skiing

Books in the "Victim's Guide" series

($4.99 £2.99 paperback)

Award winning cartoonist Roland Fiddy sees the funny side to life's phobias, nightmares and catastrophes.

The Victim's Guide to the Dentist
The Victim's Guide to the Doctor
The Victim's Guide to Middle Age

Great Britain: Order these super books from your local bookseller or from Exley Publications Ltd, 16 Chalk Hill, Watford, Herts WD1 4BN. (Please send £1.30 to cover postage and packing on 1 book, £2.60 on 2 or more books.)